The Complete Diabetic Cookbook for Beginners

1500 Days of Easy, Low-Sugar & Low-Carb
Recipes for Prediabetes and Diabetes
Types 1 and 2

By

Lorena Preston

Contents

Introduction

"Let food be thy medicine and medicine be thy food."
-Hippocrates

Welcome to Joyful Eating: Embracing Diabetic-Friendly Cooking

Welcome to "The Ultimate Cookbook for Beginners: 30 Days to Joyful Eating," where we embark on a culinary journey tailored for those managing diabetes, but with a twist of joy and simplicity. Whether you're newly diagnosed, supporting someone with diabetes, or simply seeking a healthier lifestyle, this cookbook is designed to demystify diabetic-friendly cooking without sacrificing flavor or satisfaction.

Our mission is to transform the daily task of meal preparation into an enjoyable experience, infusing a sense of joy and creativity into every dish. We believe that a diabetes diagnosis doesn't mean the end of delicious food but the beginning of a new, mindful way of cooking and eating that can be as delightful as it is nutritious.

Understanding Diabetes: Types, Management, and Diet

Diabetes, a condition characterized by elevated blood glucose levels, comes in various forms, primarily Type 1, Type 2, and gestational diabetes. Each type requires unique management strategies, but they all share a common thread—the critical role of diet in maintaining blood glucose levels.

Eating well-balanced meals, rich in nutrients, fiber, and appropriate portions, can significantly influence blood glucose control, weight management, and overall well-being. This book aims to provide you with the knowledge and tools to prepare meals that support your health goals, all while keeping your taste buds happy.

Navigating the Cookbook: How to Use This Book for Best Results

This cookbook is more than just a collection of recipes; it's a guide to transforming your relationship with food. Each recipe is crafted to be straightforward and enjoyable, with clear nutritional information to help you make informed choices.

- **Daily Meal Plans:** We've organized the book into 30 days of meal plans, each with breakfast, lunch, dinner, and snack options, to take the guesswork out of what to eat and when.

- **Step-by-Step Instructions:** Each recipe comes with easy-to-follow steps, ensuring success in the kitchen, even for the novice cook.

- **Nutritional Breakdown:** Every dish includes a detailed nutritional profile, helping you keep track of carbs, sugars, fats, and other essential nutrients.

- **Variety and Flexibility:** We understand that tastes and dietary needs vary, so we've included tips for customizing recipes to suit your preferences and dietary restrictions.

- **Empowering Knowledge:** Alongside recipes, you'll find insights on how different foods and cooking methods impact blood glucose levels, empowering you to make mindful choices beyond the cookbook.

As you turn these pages, we invite you to embrace the joy of cooking and the pleasure of eating well. Remember, this journey is not just about following recipes—it's about discovering the freedom and happiness that comes from creating nourishing, delightful meals for yourself and your loved ones. Let's begin this journey of joyful eating together

Chapter 1

The Basics of Diabetic Cooking

"One cannot think well, love well, sleep well, if one has not dined well."
-Virginia Woolf

Embark on a culinary journey where every ingredient and recipe is tailored to nourish your body and delight your palate. This chapter is designed to be your ultimate guide, equipping you with the essentials of diabetic cooking to transform your daily meals into a source of joy and health.

Essential Ingredients for a Diabetic-Friendly Kitchen

A well-stocked kitchen is your best ally in creating meals that are both delicious and supportive of your dietary needs:

- **Whole Grains:** Incorporate a variety of whole grains like barley, millet, and farro into your diet. These grains are packed with fiber, helping to slow down glucose absorption and stabilize blood sugar levels.

- **Lean Proteins:** Diversify your protein sources by including fish rich in omega-3 fatty acids, like salmon and mackerel, which are beneficial for heart health. Plant-based proteins such as lentils and chickpeas also offer fiber and protein without the fat content of meats.

- **Healthy Fats:** Look for cold-pressed oils, like flaxseed and walnut oil, which offer omega-3 fatty acids. Remember, fats are calorie-dense, so moderation is key, even with the healthy ones.

- **Vegetables and Fruits:** Emphasize non-starchy vegetables like spinach, kale, and bell peppers that provide vitamins, minerals, and fiber with minimal impact on blood sugar. When it comes to fruits, choose those with a low glycemic index, like berries and apples.

Understanding Diabetes Types and Their Dietary Needs

Dive deeper into the nutritional nuances that can help manage different types of diabetes:

1. **Type 1 Diabetes:** Beyond carbohydrate counting, understanding the glycemic index of foods can aid in more nuanced insulin management.

2. **Type 2 Diabetes:** Incorporate foods with a low glycemic load to avoid blood sugar spikes. Foods like sweet potatoes, legumes, and most fruits are excellent choices.

3. **Gestational Diabetes:** Focus on consistent, small meals throughout the day to maintain stable blood sugar levels, incorporating a balance of carbohydrates, proteins, and fats.

4. **Prediabetes:** Emphasize a diet that's rich in whole foods, minimizing refined sugars and grains, which can spike blood sugar levels and accelerate the progression to Type 2 diabetes.

Reading and Understanding Food Labels

Deciphering food labels is a skill that can significantly enhance your ability to make healthier choices:

- **Fat Content:** Understand the types of fat listed, distinguishing between healthier unsaturated fats and unhealthy saturated and trans fats.

- **Sodium:** High sodium levels can be a concern for heart health, especially in pre-packaged foods. Look for low-sodium options.

- **Additives:** Be aware of artificial sweeteners, preservatives, and flavor enhancers. Natural ingredients typically align better with a diabetic-friendly diet.

Portion Sizes and Meal Planning Basics

Mastering portion control and meal planning can transform your eating habits:

- **Detailed Guides:** Use detailed measurements for portion sizes, such as tablespoons or cups, to get accustomed to standard serving sizes.

- **Meal Planning:** Create a meal plan that includes a variety of foods to prevent boredom and ensure a broad intake of nutrients. Planning also helps in managing portion sizes and preventing overeating.

Simple Cooking Techniques for Health and Flavor

Enhance your cooking repertoire with techniques that boost flavor without compromising health:

- **Sautéing:** Use a non-stick pan with a bit of healthy oil or broth to sauté vegetables, keeping them flavorful and nutritious.

- **Roasting:** Roasting can intensify the natural sweetness and flavors of vegetables and meats without adding unhealthy fats.

- **Flavor Layering:** Build flavors with aromatics like onions, garlic, and herbs. This technique adds depth to dishes without the need for salt or sugar.

Chapter 2

Breakfasts

"Eat breakfast like a king, lunch like a prince, and dinner like a pauper."

-Adelle Davis

Berry Almond Overnight Oats

Ingredients (for 1 serving):

- 1/2 cup rolled oats

- 1/2 cup almond milk

- 1/4 cup mixed berries (such as blueberries, raspberries, and blackberries)

- 1 tablespoon almond butter

- 1 tablespoon honey or maple syrup

- 2 tablespoons chopped almonds

- 1/4 teaspoon vanilla extract

- A pinch of salt

Instructions:

1. In a mason jar or airtight container, combine the rolled oats and almond milk.

2. Add the almond butter, honey (or maple syrup), vanilla extract, and a pinch of salt. Mix well.

3. Gently fold in the mixed berries.

4. Seal the container and refrigerate overnight.

5. Before serving, stir the oats and top with chopped almonds.

How to Serve:

Enjoy cold straight from the fridge or warm it up for a cozy breakfast. Add a splash more almond milk if the oats are too thick.

Nutrition Count Per Serving:

(Approximate values) 350 calories, 14g fat, 50g carbs, 10g protein, 8g fiber.

Greek Yogurt Parfait with Nuts and Seeds

Ingredients (for 1 serving):

- 1 cup Greek yogurt

- 2 tablespoons mixed nuts (such as walnuts, almonds, and pecans), chopped

- 1 tablespoon mixed seeds (such as pumpkin seeds and sunflower seeds)

- 1/4 cup granola

- 1/2 cup mixed fresh fruits (like berries, banana slices, and kiwi)

- 1 tablespoon honey or maple syrup

Instructions:

1. In a glass or bowl, layer half of the Greek yogurt.

2. Add a layer of half the granola, nuts, seeds, and mixed fruits.

3. Repeat the layering with the remaining yogurt, granola, nuts, seeds, and fruits.

4. Drizzle the top with honey or maple syrup.

How to Serve:

Enjoy immediately, digging in to get a bit of every layer in each spoonful.

Nutrition Count Per Serving:

(Approximate values) 420 calories, 20g fat, 45g carbs, 25g protein, 6g fiber.

Whole Grain Banana Pancakes

Ingredients (for 1 serving):

- 1/2 ripe banana, mashed

- 1/2 cup whole grain flour

- 1/2 teaspoon baking powder

- 1/4 cup almond milk or any milk of choice

- 1 egg

- 1/2 teaspoon vanilla extract

- 1/2 tablespoon honey or maple syrup

- Pinch of salt

- Cooking spray or butter for the pan

- Optional toppings: sliced bananas, berries, honey, or maple syrup

Instructions:

1. In a bowl, combine the mashed banana, whole grain flour, baking powder, and a pinch of salt.

2. In another bowl, whisk together the egg, almond milk, vanilla extract, and honey (or maple syrup).

3. Pour the wet ingredients into the dry ingredients and stir until just combined. Let the batter sit for 5 minutes to thicken slightly.

4. Heat a non-stick skillet over medium heat and lightly coat with cooking spray or butter.

5. Pour small ladles of batter onto the skillet. Cook until bubbles form on the surface and the edges look set, about 2 minutes. Flip and cook for another 1-2 minutes or until golden brown.

6. Repeat with the remaining batter, adding more cooking spray or butter as needed.

How to Serve:

Serve the pancakes warm with your choice of toppings, like fresh fruit or a drizzle of honey or maple syrup.

Nutrition Count Per Serving:

(Approximate values) 350 calories, 5g fat, 60g carbs, 12g protein, 8g fiber.

Spinach and Mushroom Egg Muffins

Ingredients (for 1 serving - makes about 2 muffins):

- 2 large eggs

- 1/2 cup fresh spinach, washed and roughly chopped

- 1/4 cup sliced mushrooms

- 2 tablespoons shredded cheese (optional)

- Salt and pepper to taste

- Cooking spray or oil for greasing

Instructions:

1. Preheat your oven to 350°F (175°C) and grease a muffin tin with cooking spray or oil.

2. Beat the eggs in a bowl. Season with salt and pepper.

3. Stir in the spinach, mushrooms, and cheese (if using) into the eggs.

4. Pour the mixture into the muffin tin, filling each cup about 3/4 full.

5. Bake in the preheated oven for 20-25 minutes, or until the muffins are set and lightly golden on top.

How to Serve:

Let the muffins cool for a few minutes before removing them from the tin. They can be served warm or stored in the refrigerator for a quick breakfast option throughout the week.

Nutrition Count Per Serving (2 muffins):

(Approximate values) 220 calories, 14g fat, 4g carbs, 20g protein, 1g fiber.

Cinnamon Apple Chia Pudding

Ingredients (for 1 serving):

- 1/4 cup chia seeds

- 1 cup almond milk (or any milk of your choice)

- 1/2 apple, peeled and grated

- 1/2 teaspoon cinnamon

- 1 tablespoon maple syrup or honey

- 1/4 teaspoon vanilla extract

- Optional toppings: sliced almonds, additional grated apple, a sprinkle of cinnamon

Instructions:

1. In a bowl or jar, mix the chia seeds, almond milk, grated apple, cinnamon, maple syrup (or honey), and vanilla extract.

2. Stir well to combine. Let the mixture sit for 5 minutes, then stir again to prevent the chia seeds from clumping.

3. Cover and refrigerate for at least 2 hours or overnight until it has thickened into a pudding consistency.

4. Before serving, stir the pudding again and add a bit more milk if it's too thick.

How to Serve:

Top the chia pudding with sliced almonds, extra grated apple, and a sprinkle of cinnamon. Enjoy as a refreshing and filling breakfast.

Nutrition Count Per Serving:

(Approximate values) 300 calories, 15g fat, 40g carbs, 8g protein, 15g fiber.

Avocado and Egg Breakfast Wrap

Ingredients (for 1 serving):

- 1 large whole grain or whole wheat tortilla
- 1 egg, cooked to preference (scrambled or fried)
- 1/2 ripe avocado, sliced
- 1/4 cup fresh spinach leaves
- 2 tablespoons shredded cheese (optional)
- Salt and pepper to taste
- Optional: salsa, hot sauce, or Greek yogurt for serving

Instructions:

1. If using a scrambled egg, whisk the egg in a bowl with salt and pepper, and cook in a non-stick skillet until set. For a fried egg, cook the egg in the skillet to your preferred doneness.
2. Warm the tortilla in a skillet or microwave until flexible.
3. Place the cooked egg in the center of the tortilla.
4. Top the egg with sliced avocado, spinach, and shredded cheese.
5. Fold in the sides of the tortilla and roll it up tightly to enclose the filling.
6. Serve immediately, with salsa, hot sauce, or a dollop of Greek yogurt if desired.

How to Serve:

Enjoy the wrap as is for a handheld breakfast or cut it in half to reveal the colorful layers inside.

Nutrition Count Per Serving:

(Approximate values) 400 calories, 20g fat, 35g carbs, 18g protein, 7g fiber.

Tomato Basil Cottage Cheese Bowl

Ingredients (for 1 serving):

- 1 cup cottage cheese

- 1/2 cup cherry tomatoes, halved

- 2 tablespoons fresh basil, chopped

- Salt and pepper to taste

- 1 tablespoon balsamic glaze or vinegar (optional)

- Optional additions: sliced cucumbers, olives, or roasted red peppers

Instructions:

1. Place the cottage cheese in a serving bowl.

2. Top the cottage cheese with halved cherry tomatoes and chopped basil.

3. Season with salt and pepper to taste.

4. Drizzle with balsamic glaze or vinegar, if using.

5. Mix gently before eating, or enjoy the layers as they are.

How to Serve:

This bowl is perfect as a standalone breakfast or can be paired with whole-grain toast or crackers for added crunch.

Nutrition Count Per Serving:

(Approximate values) 220 calories, 5g fat, 15g carbs, 28g protein, 2g fiber.

Almond Butter Smoothie

Ingredients (for 1 serving):

- 1 banana, sliced and frozen

- 1 tablespoon almond butter

- 1 cup unsweetened almond milk (or any milk of your choice)

- 1/2 teaspoon vanilla extract

- 1 tablespoon flaxseed meal (optional)

- Ice cubes (optional for a thicker smoothie)

- Optional toppings: sliced almonds, a drizzle of almond butter, or banana slices

Instructions:

1. In a blender, combine the frozen banana slices, almond butter, almond milk, vanilla extract, and flaxseed meal if using.

2. Blend until smooth. If the smoothie is too thick, add more milk to reach your desired consistency. If it's too thin, add a few ice cubes and blend again.

3. Taste and adjust the sweetness or add more almond butter if desired.

How to Serve:

Pour the smoothie into a glass and garnish with sliced almonds, a drizzle of almond butter, or a few banana slices on top.

Nutrition Count Per Serving:

(Approximate values) 300 calories, 15g fat, 35g carbs, 10g protein, 7g fiber.

Sweet Potato and Kale Hash

Ingredients (for 1 serving):

- 1 medium sweet potato, peeled and diced
- 1 cup kale, washed and roughly chopped
- 1/4 cup red onion, diced
- 1 garlic clove, minced
- 2 tablespoons olive oil
- Salt and pepper to taste
- 1/4 teaspoon smoked paprika (optional)
- 1 egg (optional, for topping)
- Fresh herbs like parsley or chives for garnish (optional)

Instructions:

1. Heat olive oil in a skillet over medium heat. Add the diced sweet potatoes and sauté until they start to soften, about 5 minutes.
2. Add the diced onion and minced garlic to the skillet. Continue to cook until the onion is translucent and fragrant, about 2-3 minutes.
3. Stir in the chopped kale, and cook until it wilts and the sweet potatoes are tender, about 5 more minutes. Season with salt, pepper, and smoked paprika.
4. In a separate pan, cook an egg to your preference (fried, poached, or scrambled) if using.
5. Serve the hash in a bowl or on a plate, topped with the cooked egg and garnished with fresh herbs.

How to Serve:

This hash can be served as a hearty breakfast bowl on its own or with a slice of whole-grain toast.

Nutrition Count Per Serving:

(Approximate values without the egg) 300 calories, 14g fat, 40g carbs, 6g protein, 6g fiber.

Multigrain Blueberry Waffles

Ingredients (for 1 serving):

- 1/2 cup multigrain waffle mix (or make your own with a blend of whole wheat, oat, and cornmeal flours)
- 1/2 cup water or milk (as needed for the waffle mix)
- 1/4 cup blueberries (fresh or frozen)
- 1 tablespoon vegetable oil or melted butter
- Cooking spray for the waffle iron
- Optional: maple syrup, extra blueberries, or a dollop of Greek yogurt for serving

Instructions:

1. Preheat your waffle iron according to the manufacturer's instructions.
2. In a bowl, combine the waffle mix, water or milk, and oil or melted butter. Stir until just combined (it's okay if there are a few lumps).
3. Gently fold in the blueberries.
4. Spray the preheated waffle iron with cooking spray.
5. Pour the batter onto the waffle iron and close the lid. Cook until the waffle is golden brown and crisp, following your waffle iron's instructions.
6. Carefully remove the waffle and repeat with any remaining batter.

How to Serve:

Serve the waffles hot with your choice of toppings, such as maple syrup, additional blueberries, or a dollop of Greek yogurt.

Nutrition Count Per Serving:

(Approximate values) 350 calories, 16g fat, 45g carbs, 8g protein, 6g fiber.

Quinoa and Fruit Breakfast Bowl

Ingredients (for 1 serving):

- 1/2 cup cooked quinoa

- 1/4 cup fresh blueberries

- 1/4 cup diced strawberries

- 1/2 banana, sliced

- 1 tablespoon chopped nuts (such as almonds or walnuts)

- 1 tablespoon honey or maple syrup

- 1/4 teaspoon ground cinnamon

- 1/4 cup almond milk or any milk of your choice

Instructions:

1. In a bowl, combine the cooked quinoa, blueberries, strawberries, and banana slices.

2. Sprinkle with chopped nuts and ground cinnamon.

3. Drizzle honey or maple syrup over the top.

4. Pour almond milk around the quinoa mixture just before serving.

How to Serve:

Enjoy this nutritious and colorful breakfast bowl as a refreshing start to your day.

Nutrition Count Per Serving:

(Approximate values) 330 calories, 7g fat, 60g carbs, 8g protein, 7g fiber.

Smoked Salmon and Cream Cheese Bagel

Ingredients (for 1 serving):

- 1 whole grain bagel, halved and toasted

- 2 tablespoons cream cheese

- 2 ounces smoked salmon

- 2 thin slices of red onion

- 1 tablespoon capers

- A few slices of cucumber (optional)

- Fresh dill for garnish (optional)

- Black pepper to taste

Instructions:

1. Spread the cream cheese evenly over the two toasted bagel halves.

2. Layer the smoked salmon on top of the cream cheese.

3. Add slices of red onion, cucumber (if using), and capers.

4. Garnish with fresh dill and a sprinkle of black pepper.

How to Serve:

Serve the bagel open-faced or sandwiched together, depending on your preference.

Nutrition Count Per Serving:

(Approximate values) 400 calories, 18g fat, 44g carbs, 22g protein, 6g fiber.

Veggie-Packed Frittata

Ingredients (for 1 serving):

- 2 large eggs
- 1/4 cup diced bell peppers
- 1/4 cup chopped spinach
- 2 tablespoons diced onions
- 2 tablespoons grated cheese (your choice)
- 1 tablespoon olive oil
- Salt and pepper to taste
- Herbs like chives or parsley for garnish (optional)

Instructions:

1. Preheat the oven to 375°F (190°C) if you're using an oven-safe skillet.
2. Beat the eggs in a bowl, season with salt and pepper.
3. Heat the olive oil in a small oven-safe skillet or non-stick pan over medium heat. Sauté the onions and bell peppers until they are soft.
4. Add the chopped spinach and cook until just wilted.
5. Pour the beaten eggs over the vegetables, tilting the pan to spread them evenly. Sprinkle the cheese on top.
6. Cook without stirring for 2-3 minutes until the edges start to set.
7. Transfer the skillet to the oven (if using) and bake for 8-10 minutes or until the frittata is set and slightly golden on top. If not using an oven, cover the skillet with a lid and let the frittata cook through on the stove.

How to Serve:

Garnish with fresh herbs and serve warm, either straight from the skillet or sliced into wedges.

Nutrition Count Per Serving:

(Approximate values) 300 calories, 22g fat, 6g carbs, 18g protein, 1g fiber.

Low-Carb Blueberry Muffins

Ingredients (for 1 serving - makes about 2 muffins):

- 1/4 cup almond flour

- 1 tablespoon coconut flour

- 1/4 teaspoon baking powder

- 1 egg

- 2 tablespoons erythritol (or other sugar substitute)

- 2 tablespoons unsweetened almond milk

- 1 tablespoon melted butter or coconut oil

- 1/4 teaspoon vanilla extract

- 1/4 cup blueberries

- A pinch of salt

Instructions:

1. Preheat the oven to 350°F (175°C) and line a muffin tin with paper liners or grease with butter or oil.

2. In a bowl, mix almond flour, coconut flour, baking powder, and salt.

3. In another bowl, whisk the egg with erythritol, almond milk, melted butter (or coconut oil), and vanilla extract.

4. Combine the wet and dry ingredients, stirring until just mixed. Fold in the blueberries gently.

5. Divide the batter between the prepared muffin cups, filling each about 3/4 full.

6. Bake for 18-20 minutes, or until a toothpick inserted into the center comes out clean.

7. Let the muffins cool in the pan for a few minutes, then transfer to a wire rack to cool completely.

How to Serve:

Enjoy the muffins warm or at room temperature, perfect for a grab-and-go breakfast.

Nutrition Count Per Serving (2 muffins):

(Approximate values) 280 calories, 23g fat, 12g carbs, 10g protein, 6g fiber.

Zucchini Bread Oatmeal

Ingredients (for 1 serving):

- 1/2 cup rolled oats
- 1 cup water or milk
- 1/2 cup grated zucchini
- 1/2 teaspoon cinnamon
- 1/8 teaspoon nutmeg
- 1 tablespoon chopped walnuts or pecans
- 1 tablespoon maple syrup or honey
- 1/2 teaspoon vanilla extract
- Pinch of salt

Instructions:

1. In a small saucepan, combine the oats and water (or milk) and bring to a simmer over medium heat.

2. Add the grated zucchini, cinnamon, nutmeg, and a pinch of salt. Stir well.

3. Continue to cook, stirring occasionally, until the oats are tender and the mixture has thickened, about 5 minutes.

4. Remove from heat and stir in the vanilla extract and maple syrup (or honey).

5. Transfer to a bowl and top with chopped nuts.

How to Serve:

Enjoy this warm and comforting oatmeal as a nutritious start to your day, reminiscent of zucchini bread.

Nutrition Count Per Serving:

(Approximate values) 300 calories, 8g fat, 50g carbs, 10g protein, 6g fiber.

Savory Breakfast Quinoa with Eggs and Spinach

Ingredients (for 1 serving):

- 1/2 cup cooked quinoa

- 1 large egg

- 1 cup fresh spinach

- 1 tablespoon olive oil

- 1/4 cup diced tomatoes

- Salt and pepper to taste

- Optional: grated cheese, fresh herbs, or avocado slices for topping

Instructions:

1. Heat the olive oil in a skillet over medium heat. Add the spinach and sauté until wilted, about 2 minutes.

2. Add the cooked quinoa and diced tomatoes to the skillet. Season with salt and pepper. Stir and cook until everything is heated through.

3. Make a well in the center of the quinoa mixture and crack the egg into it. Cover the skillet and cook until the egg white is set but the yolk is still runny, or to your desired doneness.

4. Remove from heat and transfer to a plate.

How to Serve:

Serve hot with optional toppings like grated cheese, fresh herbs, or slices of avocado.

Nutrition Count Per Serving:

(Approximate values) 350 calories, 20g fat, 30g carbs, 15g protein, 5g fiber.

Nutty Granola with Unsweetened Yogurt

Ingredients (for 1 serving):

- 1/2 cup homemade or store-bought nutty granola (mix of oats, almonds, walnuts, and pumpkin seeds)

- 1 cup unsweetened Greek yogurt

- 1 tablespoon honey or maple syrup (optional)

- 1/4 cup fresh berries (such as strawberries, blueberries, or raspberries)

Instructions:

1. In a serving bowl, layer the Greek yogurt at the bottom.

2. Top the yogurt with the nutty granola.

3. Add the fresh berries on top of the granola.

4. Drizzle with honey or maple syrup if a touch of sweetness is desired.

How to Serve:

Enjoy this parfait-style breakfast as a wholesome start to your day, offering a good balance of protein, healthy fats, and fiber.

Nutrition Count Per Serving:

(Approximate values) 400 calories, 20g fat, 35g carbs, 25g protein, 5g fiber.

Breakfast Tofu Scramble with Peppers

Ingredients (for 1 serving):

- 1/2 block firm tofu, crumbled

- 1/4 cup diced bell peppers (any color)

- 1/4 cup diced onions

- 2 tablespoons nutritional yeast (for a cheesy flavor)

- 1/2 teaspoon turmeric (for color)

- 1 tablespoon olive oil

- Salt and pepper to taste

- Fresh herbs like parsley or chives for garnish

Instructions:

1. Heat the olive oil in a skillet over medium heat.

2. Add the onions and bell peppers, sautéing until they are soft.

3. Add the crumbled tofu, turmeric, nutritional yeast, salt, and pepper. Stir well to combine.

4. Cook the mixture for 5-7 minutes, stirring occasionally, until the tofu is heated through and starts to get a slightly golden color.

5. Adjust seasoning to taste.

How to Serve:

Garnish with fresh herbs and serve hot as a hearty and satisfying plant-based breakfast option.

Nutrition Count Per Serving:

(Approximate values) 300 calories, 20g fat, 10g carbs, 20g protein, 4g fiber.

Pumpkin Spice Protein Shake

Ingredients (for 1 serving):

- 1 scoop vanilla protein powder

- 1/2 cup pumpkin puree (canned or fresh)

- 1 cup almond milk (or any milk of your choice)

- 1/2 banana (preferably frozen for a thicker texture)

- 1/2 teaspoon pumpkin pie spice

- 1 tablespoon maple syrup or honey (optional, depending on the sweetness of your protein powder)

- Ice cubes (optional, for a colder shake)

Instructions:

1. Combine the protein powder, pumpkin puree, almond milk, banana, pumpkin pie spice, and maple syrup (if using) in a blender.

2. Add a few ice cubes if you prefer a colder shake.

3. Blend until smooth and creamy.

4. Taste and adjust the sweetness or spice as desired.

How to Serve:

Pour the shake into a glass and enjoy immediately, perhaps with a sprinkle of cinnamon or extra pumpkin pie spice on top.

Nutrition Count Per Serving:

(Approximate values) 300 calories, 3g fat, 40g carbs, 28g protein, 5g fiber.

Apple Cinnamon Breakfast Bars

Ingredients (for 1 serving - makes multiple bars, store the rest):

- 1 cup rolled oats
- 1/2 cup whole wheat flour
- 1/4 cup apple sauce
- 1 apple, peeled, cored, and finely diced
- 1/4 cup honey or maple syrup
- 1/2 teaspoon baking soda
- 1 teaspoon cinnamon
- Pinch of salt
- 1/4 cup raisins or nuts (optional)

Instructions:

1. Preheat the oven to 350°F (175°C) and line a baking dish with parchment paper.
2. In a large bowl, mix the oats, whole wheat flour, baking soda, cinnamon, and salt.
3. Stir in the apple sauce, honey (or maple syrup), and diced apple until well combined. Fold in raisins or nuts if using.
4. Spread the mixture evenly in the prepared baking dish, pressing down firmly.
5. Bake for 20-25 minutes, or until the edges are golden brown and the center is set.
6. Let the bars cool in the dish before cutting into portions.

How to Serve:

Enjoy a bar as a quick and nutritious breakfast option, perfect for on-the-go mornings.

Nutrition Count Per Serving (1 bar if cut into 8):

(Approximate values) 150 calories, 2g fat, 30g carbs, 4g protein, 3g fiber.

Chapter 3

Light Bites & Snacks

"Small helpings, no seconds, a little bit of everything, no snacking, and a bit of wine at dinner. It's French. It is moderation itself."

-Julia Child

Cucumber Hummus Bites

Ingredients (for 1 serving):

- 1 large cucumber, sliced into rounds

- 1/2 cup hummus

- Paprika, for garnish

- Fresh parsley, chopped (for garnish)

Instructions:

1. Slice the cucumber into round discs, about 1/4 inch thick.

2. Spoon a small amount of hummus onto each cucumber slice.

3. Sprinkle a dash of paprika and some chopped parsley on top of the hummus for garnish.

How to Serve:

Arrange the cucumber hummus bites on a plate and serve as a refreshing and healthy snack.

Nutrition Count Per Serving:

Approximately: 150 calories, 9g fat, 13g carbs, 7g protein, 5g fiber.

Roasted Spiced Nuts

Ingredients (for 1 serving):

- 1/2 cup mixed nuts (almonds, walnuts, pecans)

- 1/2 teaspoon olive oil

- 1/4 teaspoon each of cumin, paprika, and chili powder

- Salt to taste

Instructions:

1. Preheat the oven to 350°F (175°C).

2. In a bowl, toss the nuts with olive oil, cumin, paprika, chili powder, and salt.

3. Spread the nuts on a baking sheet in a single layer.

4. Bake for 10-15 minutes, stirring occasionally, until they are golden and fragrant.

How to Serve:

Let the nuts cool before serving. They can be enjoyed as a standalone snack or as a topping for salads.

Nutrition Count Per Serving:

Approximately: 300 calories, 26g fat, 12g carbs, 8g protein, 4g fiber.

Baked Zucchini Chips

Ingredients (for 1 serving):

- 1 zucchini, thinly sliced

- 1 tablespoon olive oil

- Salt and pepper to taste

Instructions:

1. Preheat the oven to 375°F (190°C) and line a baking sheet with parchment paper.

2. Toss the zucchini slices with olive oil, salt, and pepper.

3. Arrange the slices in a single layer on the baking sheet.

4. Bake for 20-30 minutes, flipping halfway through, until the chips are golden and crispy.

How to Serve:

Enjoy the zucchini chips as a crunchy, low-calorie snack.

Nutrition Count Per Serving:

Approximately: 120 calories, 14g fat, 10g carbs, 2g protein, 4g fiber.

Chickpea and Avocado Salad

Ingredients (for 1 serving):

- 1/2 cup chickpeas, rinsed and drained

- 1/2 ripe avocado, diced

- 1/4 cup cherry tomatoes, halved

- 1 tablespoon lemon juice

- Salt and pepper to taste

- 1 tablespoon chopped cilantro or parsley

Instructions:

1. In a bowl, combine the chickpeas, avocado, cherry tomatoes, lemon juice, salt, and pepper.

2. Gently mix the ingredients, being careful not to mash the avocado.

3. Garnish with chopped cilantro or parsley.

How to Serve:

Serve the salad chilled as a nutritious and filling snack or light lunch.

Nutrition Count Per Serving:

Approximately: 250 calories, 15g fat, 27g carbs, 7g protein, 10g fiber.

Peanut Butter Energy Balls

Ingredients (for 1 serving - makes about 4 balls):

- 1/4 cup oats

- 2 tablespoons natural peanut butter

- 1 tablespoon honey or maple syrup

- 1 tablespoon flax seeds

- 1 tablespoon chocolate chips (optional)

Instructions:

1. In a bowl, mix together oats, peanut butter, honey or maple syrup, flax seeds, and chocolate chips if using.

2. Roll the mixture into small balls, about the size of a walnut.

3. Place the balls on a plate and refrigerate for at least 30 minutes to set.

How to Serve:

Enjoy these energy balls as a quick snack or pre-workout energy boost.

Nutrition Count Per Serving (4 balls):

Approximately: 300 calories, 18g fat, 28g carbs, 8g protein, 4g fiber.

Carrot and Raisin Pinwheels

Ingredients (for 1 serving):

- 1 large whole wheat tortilla

- 2 tablespoons cream cheese, softened

- 1/4 cup grated carrot

- 1 tablespoon raisins

- A pinch of cinnamon

Instructions:

1. Spread the cream cheese evenly over the tortilla.

2. Sprinkle the grated carrot and raisins evenly over the cream cheese.

3. Add a pinch of cinnamon for flavor.

4. Carefully roll up the tortilla tightly, then slice into 1-inch pinwheels.

How to Serve:

Arrange the pinwheels on a plate, spiral side up, as a colorful and tasty snack.

Nutrition Count Per Serving:

Approximately: 250 calories, 12g fat, 33g carbs, 6g protein, 4g fiber.

Red Pepper and Walnut Dip

Ingredients (for 1 serving):

- 1/2 cup roasted red peppers, drained

- 1/4 cup walnuts

- 1 garlic clove

- 1 tablespoon olive oil

- Salt and pepper to taste

Instructions:

1. Blend the roasted red peppers, walnuts, garlic, and olive oil in a food processor until smooth.

2. Season with salt and pepper to taste.

3. Transfer to a serving bowl.

How to Serve:

Enjoy the dip with vegetable sticks, crackers, or as a spread on toast.

Nutrition Count Per Serving:

Approximately: 300 calories, 25g fat, 15g carbs, 6g protein, 3g fiber.

Stuffed Cherry Tomatoes with Goat Cheese

Ingredients (for 1 serving):

- 8 cherry tomatoes

- 1/4 cup soft goat cheese

- Fresh herbs (like basil or parsley), finely chopped

- Salt and pepper to taste

Instructions:

1. Slice the tops off the cherry tomatoes and carefully scoop out the seeds with a small spoon.

2. Mix the goat cheese with the herbs, salt, and pepper.

3. Fill each tomato with the goat cheese mixture.

How to Serve:

Serve the stuffed tomatoes as a bite-sized appetizer or a healthy snack.

Nutrition Count Per Serving:

Approximately: 150 calories, 10g fat, 8g carbs, 8g protein, 2g fiber.

Baked Apple Slices with Cinnamon

Ingredients (for 1 serving):

- 1 apple, cored and thinly sliced

- 1/2 teaspoon ground cinnamon

- A drizzle of honey (optional)

Instructions:

1. Preheat the oven to 350°F (175°C).

2. Arrange the apple slices in a single layer on a baking sheet.

3. Sprinkle cinnamon over the slices and drizzle with honey if desired.

4. Bake for 10-15 minutes or until the apples are tender and slightly crispy at the edges.

How to Serve:

Enjoy these as a sweet, healthy snack or dessert.

Nutrition Count Per Serving:

Approximately: 100 calories, 0g fat, 26g carbs, 0g protein, 4g fiber.

Crunchy Edamame Popcorn

Ingredients (for 1 serving):

- 1/2 cup frozen edamame (shelled)

- 1 teaspoon olive oil

- Salt to taste

- A pinch of garlic powder (optional)

Instructions:

1. Preheat the oven to 375°F (190°C).

2. Toss the edamame with olive oil, salt, and garlic powder if using.

3. Spread the edamame in a single layer on a baking sheet.

4. Bake for 15-20 minutes or until crispy, stirring halfway through.

How to Serve:

Serve the edamame warm as a crunchy, protein-packed snack.

Nutrition Count Per Serving:

Approximately: 150 calories, 8g fat, 9g carbs, 12g protein, 4g fiber.

Chapter 4

Salads and Sides

"When you have the best and tastiest ingredients, you can cook very simply and the food will be extraordinary because it tastes like what it is."

-Alice Waters

Mediterranean Chickpea Salad

Ingredients (for 1 serving):

- 1/2 cup canned chickpeas, rinsed and drained

- 1/4 cup diced cucumber
- 1/4 cup halved cherry tomatoes
- 1/4 cup diced red bell pepper
- 2 tablespoons crumbled feta cheese
- 1 tablespoon chopped red onion
- 1 tablespoon olive oil
- 1 teaspoon lemon juice
- Salt and black pepper to taste
- 1/2 teaspoon dried oregano

Instructions:

1. In a bowl, combine chickpeas, cucumber, cherry tomatoes, red bell pepper, and red onion.
2. Drizzle with olive oil and lemon juice. Season with salt, pepper, and oregano.
3. Toss everything together until well mixed.
4. Sprinkle feta cheese on top before serving.

How to Serve:

Serve chilled or at room temperature as a refreshing and protein-packed side salad.

Nutrition Count Per Serving:

Approximately: 250 calories, 15g fat, 23g carbs, 9g protein, 6g fiber.

Broccoli and Cauliflower Salad with Lemon Dressing

Ingredients (for 1 serving):

- 1/2 cup broccoli florets

- 1/2 cup cauliflower florets

- 1 tablespoon olive oil

- 1 teaspoon lemon zest

- 2 tablespoons lemon juice

- Salt and pepper to taste

- 1 tablespoon chopped almonds or walnuts (optional)

Instructions:

1. Steam the broccoli and cauliflower florets until just tender, then cool them down.

2. In a small bowl, whisk together olive oil, lemon zest, lemon juice, salt, and pepper to create the dressing.

3. Toss the cooled broccoli and cauliflower in the dressing.

4. Add nuts if using, and toss again.

How to Serve:

Enjoy this vibrant side dish alongside your favorite protein, or incorporate it into a larger salad meal.

Nutrition Count Per Serving:

Approximately: 180 calories, 14g fat, 12g carbs, 4g protein, 5g fiber.

Spicy Southwest Black Bean Salad

Ingredients (for 1 serving):

- 1/2 cup black beans, rinsed and drained

- 1/4 cup corn kernels (fresh, canned, or thawed from frozen)

- 1/4 cup diced tomatoes

- 1/4 cup diced red bell pepper

- 1 tablespoon finely chopped red onion

- 1 tablespoon chopped fresh cilantro

- 1 tablespoon lime juice

- 1/4 teaspoon chili powder

- Salt and pepper to taste

Instructions:

1. Combine black beans, corn, tomatoes, red bell pepper, and red onion in a bowl.

2. Add lime juice, chili powder, salt, and pepper.

3. Toss the salad with chopped cilantro.

How to Serve:

This salad is perfect as a standalone dish or as a flavorful side to complement grilled meats or vegetables.

Nutrition Count Per Serving:

Approximately: 200 calories, 2g fat, 36g carbs, 10g protein, 10g fiber.

Rainbow Quinoa Salad

Ingredients (for 1 serving):

- 1/2 cup cooked quinoa

- 1/4 cup diced red bell pepper

- 1/4 cup shredded carrots

- 1/4 cup chopped cucumber

- 1/4 cup halved cherry tomatoes

- 2 tablespoons chopped fresh parsley

- 1 tablespoon lemon juice

- 1 tablespoon olive oil

- Salt and pepper to taste

Instructions:

1. In a bowl, mix the cooked quinoa with red bell pepper, carrots, cucumber, and cherry tomatoes.

2. Add lemon juice, olive oil, salt, and pepper, and toss well.

3. Garnish with fresh parsley before serving.

How to Serve:

Serve this colorful salad as a nutritious side or a light main dish.

Nutrition Count Per Serving:

Approximately: 250 calories, 14g fat, 30g carbs, 6g protein, 5g fiber.

Garlic Roasted Brussels Sprouts

Ingredients (for 1 serving):

- 1 cup Brussels sprouts, halved

- 1 tablespoon olive oil

- 1-2 cloves garlic, minced

- Salt and pepper to taste

Instructions:

1. Preheat the oven to 400°F (200°C).

2. Toss Brussels sprouts with olive oil, garlic, salt, and pepper.

3. Spread them out on a baking sheet, cut side down.

4. Roast for 20-25 minutes or until golden and crispy on the edges.

How to Serve:

Serve hot as a savory side dish, perfect with any main course.

Nutrition Count Per Serving:

Approximately: 140 calories, 10g fat, 12g carbs, 4g protein, 4g fiber.

Classic Greek Salad with Reduced-Fat Feta

Ingredients (for 1 serving):

- 1/2 cup cucumber, sliced

- 1/2 cup cherry tomatoes, halved

- 1/4 cup red onion, thinly sliced

- 1/4 cup reduced-fat feta cheese, crumbled

- 10 Kalamata olives, pitted and halved

- 1 tablespoon olive oil

- 1 tablespoon red wine vinegar

- Salt and pepper to taste

- 1/2 teaspoon dried oregano

Instructions:

1. In a bowl, combine cucumber, cherry tomatoes, red onion, feta cheese, and olives.

2. Drizzle with olive oil and red wine vinegar.

3. Season with salt, pepper, and oregano, then toss gently to combine.

How to Serve:

Serve this salad as a fresh and flavorful side dish or light main course.

Nutrition Count Per Serving:

Approximately: 250 calories, 20g fat, 15g carbs, 7g protein, 3g fiber.

Tangy Cucumber Salad

Ingredients (for 1 serving):

- 1 large cucumber, thinly sliced

- 1/4 cup red onion, thinly sliced

- 2 tablespoons white vinegar

- 1 tablespoon water

- 1 teaspoon sugar

- Salt and pepper to taste

- Fresh dill, chopped (optional)

Instructions:

1. Combine vinegar, water, sugar, salt, and pepper in a bowl, stirring until sugar dissolves.

2. Add cucumber and red onion slices to the dressing. Toss to coat.

3. Refrigerate for at least 30 minutes to allow flavors to meld.

How to Serve:

Garnish with fresh dill before serving, if desired.

Nutrition Count Per Serving:

Approximately: 50 calories, 0g fat, 12g carbs, 1g protein, 2g fiber.

Sautéed Green Beans with Almonds

Ingredients (for 1 serving):

- 1 cup green beans, trimmed

- 1 tablespoon olive oil

- 1 garlic clove, minced

- 2 tablespoons sliced almonds

- Salt and pepper to taste

Instructions:

1. Heat olive oil in a skillet over medium heat.

2. Add garlic and almonds, sautéing until almonds are lightly toasted.

3. Add green beans, salt, and pepper. Cook, stirring frequently, until beans are tender-crisp.

How to Serve:

Serve immediately as a crunchy and flavorful side dish.

Nutrition Count Per Serving:

Approximately: 200 calories, 15g fat, 14g carbs, 5g protein, 4g fiber.

Roasted Beet and Goat Cheese Salad

Ingredients (for 1 serving):

- 1 medium beet, peeled and diced

- 1 tablespoon olive oil

- Salt and pepper to taste

- 2 cups mixed salad greens

- 2 tablespoons crumbled goat cheese

- 1 tablespoon walnuts, chopped

- 1 tablespoon balsamic vinegar

Instructions:

1. Preheat oven to 400°F (200°C). Toss diced beet with olive oil, salt, and pepper. Roast until tender, about 25-30 minutes.

2. Let beets cool, then mix with salad greens, goat cheese, and walnuts.

3. Drizzle with balsamic vinegar before serving.

How to Serve:

Enjoy this salad as a hearty side or a light vegetarian meal.

Nutrition Count Per Serving:

Approximately: 300 calories, 20g fat, 20g carbs, 8g protein, 5g fiber.

Carrot and Cabbage Coleslaw

Ingredients (for 1 serving):

- 1/2 cup shredded green cabbage

- 1/2 cup shredded carrot

- 1 tablespoon mayonnaise

- 1 tablespoon apple cider vinegar

- 1 teaspoon honey

- Salt and pepper to taste

- Fresh herbs like parsley, chopped (optional)

Instructions:

1. In a bowl, mix mayonnaise, apple cider vinegar, honey, salt, and pepper to create the dressing.

2. Add shredded cabbage and carrot to the dressing. Toss to combine.

3. Refrigerate for at least 15 minutes before serving to allow flavors to blend.

How to Serve:

Serve chilled as a crunchy and refreshing side dish.

Nutrition Count Per Serving:

Approximately: 120 calories, 7g fat, 14g carbs, 1g protein, 3g fiber.

Chapter 5

Soups and Stews

"Only the pure in heart can make a good soup."
-Ludwig van Beethoven

Lentil and Spinach Soup

Ingredients (for 1 serving):

- 1/2 cup dried lentils, rinsed

- 2 cups vegetable broth

- 1/2 cup fresh spinach, roughly chopped

- 1/4 onion, diced

- 1 garlic clove, minced

- 1 carrot, diced

- 1/2 teaspoon ground cumin

- Salt and pepper to taste

- 1 tablespoon olive oil

Instructions:

1. Heat olive oil in a pot over medium heat. Sauté onion, garlic, and carrot until softened.

2. Add lentils and vegetable broth. Bring to a boil, then reduce heat and simmer until lentils are tender, about 20-25 minutes.

3. Stir in spinach and cumin during the last 5 minutes of cooking.

4. Season with salt and pepper to taste.

How to Serve:

Serve hot, garnished with a drizzle of olive oil or lemon juice if desired.

Nutrition Count Per Serving:

Approximately: 320 calories, 8g fat, 48g carbs, 18g protein, 15g fiber.

Tomato Basil Soup

Ingredients (for 1 serving):

- 1 cup canned tomatoes, crushed

- 1/2 onion, diced

- 1 garlic clove, minced

- 1 cup vegetable broth

- 1/4 cup fresh basil, chopped

- 1 tablespoon olive oil

- Salt and pepper to taste

- 1 tablespoon heavy cream or coconut cream (optional)

Instructions:

1. In a pot, heat olive oil over medium heat. Sauté onion and garlic until translucent.

2. Add tomatoes and vegetable broth. Simmer for 15-20 minutes.

3. Stir in fresh basil and cook for an additional 2 minutes.

4. Puree the soup using a blender or immersion blender until smooth. Return to pot.

5. Season with salt and pepper. Stir in cream if using.

How to Serve:

Enjoy warm, topped with additional fresh basil or a dollop of cream.

Nutrition Count Per Serving:

Approximately: 200 calories, 14g fat, 16g carbs, 3g protein, 4g fiber.

Butternut Squash and Carrot Soup

Ingredients (for 1 serving):

- 1 cup butternut squash, peeled and cubed

- 1/2 cup carrots, diced

- 1/2 onion, diced

- 1 garlic clove, minced

- 1 1/2 cups vegetable broth

- 1/2 teaspoon ginger, grated

- 1/2 teaspoon cinnamon

- Salt and pepper to taste

- 1 tablespoon olive oil

Instructions:

1. In a pot, heat olive oil over medium heat. Sauté onion, garlic, carrots, and squash until slightly softened.

2. Add ginger, cinnamon, and vegetable broth. Bring to a boil, then simmer until vegetables are tender.

3. Puree the mixture until smooth.

4. Season with salt and pepper.

How to Serve:

Serve the soup warm, garnished with a sprinkle of cinnamon or fresh herbs if desired.

Nutrition Count Per Serving:

Approximately: 180 calories, 7g fat, 30g carbs, 3g protein, 6g fiber.

Chicken and Vegetable Stew

Ingredients (for 1 serving):

- 1 chicken breast, diced

- 1/2 cup diced carrots

- 1/2 cup diced potatoes

- 1/4 cup diced celery

- 1/4 onion, diced

- 2 cups chicken broth

- 1/2 teaspoon thyme

- Salt and pepper to taste

- 1 tablespoon olive oil

Instructions:

1. In a pot, heat olive oil over medium heat. Cook chicken until browned.

2. Add onions, carrots, celery, and potatoes. Sauté until slightly softened.

3. Pour in chicken broth. Add thyme, salt, and pepper.

4. Bring to a boil, then simmer until vegetables are tender and chicken is fully cooked.

How to Serve:

Serve the stew hot, garnished with fresh parsley or thyme if desired.

Nutrition Count Per Serving:

Approximately: 300 calories, 9g fat, 30g carbs, 25g protein, 6g fiber.

Minestrone with Zucchini Noodles

Ingredients (for 1 serving):

- 1 cup vegetable broth
- 1/4 cup canned diced tomatoes
- 1/4 cup zucchini, spiralized into noodles
- 1/4 cup chopped spinach
- 1/4 cup cannellini beans, rinsed and drained
- 1/4 onion, diced
- 1 garlic clove, minced
- 1/2 carrot, diced
- 1/2 teaspoon Italian seasoning
- Salt and pepper to taste
- 1 tablespoon olive oil

Instructions:

1. In a pot, heat olive oil over medium heat. Sauté onion, garlic, and carrot until softened.
2. Add vegetable broth, diced tomatoes, cannellini beans, and Italian seasoning. Simmer for 10-15 minutes.
3. Add zucchini noodles and spinach. Cook for an additional 2-3 minutes.
4. Season with salt and pepper.

How to Serve:

Enjoy this light and nutritious soup hot, sprinkled with grated Parmesan if desired.

Nutrition Count Per Serving:

Approximately: 220 calories, 8g fat, 28g carbs, 8g protein, 8g fiber.

Beef and Barley Soup

Ingredients (for 1 serving):

- 1/2 cup cooked beef, cubed

- 1/4 cup barley

- 1 cup beef broth

- 1/4 cup diced carrots

- 1/4 cup diced celery

- 1/4 onion, diced

- 1 garlic clove, minced

- 1/2 teaspoon thyme

- Salt and pepper to taste

- 1 tablespoon olive oil

Instructions:

1. Heat olive oil in a pot over medium heat. Sauté onion and garlic until translucent.

2. Add carrots, celery, beef, and barley. Stir for a couple of minutes.

3. Pour in beef broth and add thyme. Season with salt and pepper.

4. Bring to a boil, then simmer until barley is cooked and vegetables are tender, about 30 minutes.

How to Serve:

Serve warm, with a sprinkle of fresh parsley if desired.

Nutrition Count Per Serving:

Approximately: 350 calories, 15g fat, 30g carbs, 20g protein, 6g fiber.

Spiced Pumpkin Soup

Ingredients (for 1 serving):

- 1 cup pumpkin puree (not pie filling)

- 1 cup vegetable broth

- 1/4 cup coconut milk

- 1/2 onion, diced

- 1 garlic clove, minced

- 1/2 teaspoon curry powder

- 1/4 teaspoon cinnamon

- Salt and pepper to taste

- 1 tablespoon olive oil

Instructions:

1. In a pot, heat olive oil over medium heat. Sauté onion and garlic until soft.

2. Add pumpkin puree, vegetable broth, curry powder, and cinnamon. Stir well.

3. Bring to a simmer and cook for about 10 minutes.

4. Stir in coconut milk and heat through. Season with salt and pepper.

How to Serve:

Serve hot, garnished with a swirl of coconut milk or pumpkin seeds.

Nutrition Count Per Serving:

Approximately: 250 calories, 15g fat, 28g carbs, 5g protein, 7g fiber.

Turkey Chili

Ingredients (for 1 serving):

- 1/2 lb ground turkey

- 1/2 cup canned tomatoes, crushed

- 1/4 cup kidney beans, rinsed and drained

- 1/4 onion, diced

- 1 garlic clove, minced

- 1/2 teaspoon chili powder

- 1/4 teaspoon cumin

- Salt and pepper to taste

- 1 tablespoon olive oil

Instructions:

1. Heat olive oil in a pot over medium heat. Cook the turkey until browned.

2. Add onion and garlic, sautéing until soft.

3. Stir in chili powder, cumin, tomatoes, and kidney beans. Season with salt and pepper.

4. Simmer for at least 20 minutes, allowing flavors to meld.

How to Serve:

Enjoy hot, topped with a dollop of low-fat sour cream or shredded cheese if desired.

Nutrition Count Per Serving:

Approximately: 300 calories, 12g fat, 20g carbs, 30g protein, 6g fiber.

Mushroom and Wild Rice Soup

Ingredients (for 1 serving):

- 1/2 cup wild rice, cooked
- 1 cup mushrooms, sliced
- 1/4 onion, diced
- 1 garlic clove, minced
- 1 cup vegetable broth
- 1/4 cup heavy cream or almond milk
- 1/2 teaspoon thyme
- Salt and pepper to taste
- 1 tablespoon olive oil

Instructions:

1. In a pot, heat olive oil over medium heat. Sauté onion, garlic, and mushrooms until the mushrooms are browned and soft.

2. Add vegetable broth, thyme, and cooked wild rice. Bring to a simmer.

3. Cook for about 10 minutes. Stir in cream or almond milk, heating through.

4. Season with salt and pepper.

How to Serve:

Serve warm, garnished with fresh herbs or a sprinkle of grated Parmesan.

Nutrition Count Per Serving:

Approximately: 250 calories, 15g fat, 25g carbs, 8g protein, 4g fiber.

Creamy Cauliflower Soup

Ingredients (for 1 serving):

- 1 cup cauliflower florets

- 1 cup almond milk

- 1/2 onion, diced

- 1 garlic clove, minced

- 1/2 cup vegetable broth

- Salt and pepper to taste

- 1 tablespoon olive oil

Instructions:

1. In a pot, heat olive oil over medium heat. Sauté onion and garlic until translucent.

2. Add cauliflower and vegetable broth. Cover and simmer until cauliflower is tender.

3. Blend the mixture with almond milk until smooth. Return to pot to heat through.

4. Season with salt and pepper.

How to Serve:

Enjoy the soup warm, garnished with a drizzle of olive oil or a sprinkle of fresh herbs.

Nutrition Count Per Serving:

Approximately: 180 calories, 12g fat, 16g carbs, 6g protein, 4g fiber.

Chapter 6

Main Courses

"A recipe has no soul. You, as the cook, must bring soul to the recipe."

-Thomas Keller

Eggplant Lasagna with Spinach and Ricotta

Ingredients (for 1 serving):

- 1 medium eggplant, sliced lengthwise

- 1/2 cup ricotta cheese

- 1/2 cup spinach, cooked and drained

- 1 cup tomato sauce

- 1/4 cup shredded mozzarella cheese

- 1 garlic clove, minced

- Salt and pepper to taste

- Olive oil for brushing

Instructions:

1. Preheat the oven to 375°F (190°C). Brush eggplant slices with olive oil and season with salt and pepper. Bake for 20 minutes or until tender.

2. Mix ricotta cheese, spinach, and minced garlic in a bowl. Season with salt and pepper.

3. In a baking dish, layer an eggplant slice, spread some ricotta mixture, and then tomato sauce. Repeat layers.

4. Top with shredded mozzarella cheese.

5. Bake for 25-30 minutes, or until cheese is bubbly and golden.

How to Serve:

Serve warm as a hearty and nutritious vegetarian main course.

Nutrition Count Per Serving:

Approximately: 400 calories, 20g fat, 35g carbs, 20g protein, 10g fiber.

Quinoa Stuffed Bell Peppers

Ingredients (for 1 serving):

- 1 large bell pepper, halved and seeded

- 1/2 cup cooked quinoa

- 1/4 cup black beans, rinsed and drained

- 1/4 cup corn kernels

- 1/4 cup diced tomatoes

- 1/4 cup shredded cheese (optional)

- 1 tablespoon chopped cilantro

- Salt and pepper to taste

Instructions:

1. Preheat the oven to 350°F (175°C).

2. Mix quinoa, black beans, corn, tomatoes, and cilantro in a bowl. Season with salt and pepper.

3. Stuff the bell pepper halves with the quinoa mixture and top with cheese if using.

4. Place in a baking dish and bake for 30 minutes or until the peppers are tender.

How to Serve:

Serve the stuffed peppers hot, garnished with additional cilantro or avocado slices.

Nutrition Count Per Serving:

Approximately: 350 calories, 9g fat, 53g carbs, 15g protein, 10g fiber.

Baked Spaghetti Squash with Tomato Sauce

Ingredients (for 1 serving):

- 1/2 spaghetti squash

- 1 cup tomato sauce

- 1/4 cup shredded mozzarella cheese

- 1 garlic clove, minced

- Salt and pepper to taste

- Olive oil

Instructions:

1. Preheat the oven to 400°F (200°C). Cut the squash in half, remove seeds, brush with olive oil, and season with salt and pepper.

2. Place squash cut-side down on a baking sheet. Bake for 40 minutes or until tender.

3. Use a fork to scrape the squash strands into a bowl.

4. Mix spaghetti squash strands with tomato sauce and minced garlic.

5. Return the mixture to the squash shell, top with mozzarella, and bake until the cheese is melted and bubbly.

How to Serve:

Serve warm, directly in the squash shell for a fun and nutritious meal.

Nutrition Count Per Serving:

Approximately: 300 calories, 12g fat, 45g carbs, 10g protein, 8g fiber.

Lentil Loaf with Tomato Glaze

Ingredients (for 1 serving):

- 1/2 cup cooked lentils

- 1/4 cup breadcrumbs

- 1/4 onion, finely chopped

- 1 garlic clove, minced

- 1/4 carrot, grated

- 1 egg, beaten

- 1/4 cup tomato sauce for glaze

- Salt and pepper to taste

Instructions:

1. Preheat the oven to 350°F (175°C).

2. In a bowl, combine lentils, breadcrumbs, onion, garlic, carrot, and egg. Season with salt and pepper.

3. Press the mixture into a small loaf pan.

4. Spread tomato sauce on top as a glaze.

5. Bake for 40-45 minutes or until firm and cooked through.

How to Serve:

Slice the lentil loaf and serve warm, possibly with additional tomato sauce or a side salad.

Nutrition Count Per Serving:

Approximately: 320 calories, 8g fat, 45g carbs, 20g protein, 10g fiber.

Zucchini Noodles with Pesto

Ingredients (for 1 serving):

- 1 large zucchini, spiralized into noodles

- 2 tablespoons pesto sauce

- 1 tablespoon pine nuts, toasted

- 1 tablespoon grated Parmesan cheese

- Salt and pepper to taste

Instructions:

1. Heat the zucchini noodles in a skillet over medium heat for 2-3 minutes, just until tender.

2. Remove from heat and toss with pesto sauce.

3. Season with salt and pepper.

How to Serve:

Top with toasted pine nuts and grated Parmesan cheese before serving.

Nutrition Count Per Serving:

Approximately: 250 calories, 20g fat, 10g carbs, 7g protein, 3g fiber.

Cauliflower Steaks with Herb Salsa

Ingredients (for 1 serving):

- 2 cauliflower steaks (1-inch thick slices)
- 1 tablespoon olive oil or unsalted butter
- Salt and pepper, to taste
- 1/4 cup fresh herbs (parsley, cilantro, basil), finely chopped
- 2 tablespoons olive oil (for salsa)
- 1/4 teaspoon nutmeg (optional)
- 1 tablespoon lemon juice
- Salt and pepper to taste
- 1/4 cup diced tomatoes (for garnish)
- 1 tablespoon chopped fresh basil (for garnish)

Instructions:

1. Season the cauliflower steaks with salt, pepper, and optional nutmeg.
2. Heat olive oil or butter in a non-stick skillet over medium heat.
3. Add the cauliflower steaks to the skillet and cook until each side is golden brown, approximately 5 minutes per side.
4. In a bowl, mix the chopped herbs, 2 tablespoons of olive oil, lemon juice, salt, and pepper to create the salsa.
5. Once the cauliflower is cooked, place it on a serving plate.
6. Top the cauliflower steaks with the herb salsa.
7. Garnish with diced tomatoes and chopped basil.

How to Serve:

Enjoy this dish as a main course, paired with a side salad or your choice of protein for a balanced meal.

Nutrition Count Per Serving:

Approximately: 310 calories, 22g fat, 8g carbs, 22g protein, 3g fiber.

Black Bean and Sweet Potato Enchiladas

Ingredients (for 1 serving):

- 1/2 medium sweet potato, cubed
- 1/2 cup black beans, rinsed and drained
- 2 small corn tortillas
- 1/2 cup enchilada sauce
- 1/4 cup shredded cheese (optional)
- 1 tablespoon olive oil or unsalted butter
- Salt and pepper, to taste
- 1/4 cup diced tomatoes (for garnish)
- 1 tablespoon chopped fresh cilantro (for garnish)

Instructions:

1. Preheat the oven to 375°F (190°C). Toss sweet potato cubes with olive oil or melted butter, salt, and pepper, and roast until tender.
2. Mix the roasted sweet potatoes with black beans.
3. Fill the tortillas with the sweet potato and bean mixture, roll them up, and place in a baking dish.
4. Pour enchilada sauce over the filled tortillas and top with cheese if using.
5. Bake in the oven until the cheese is melted and the edges of the tortillas are slightly crispy.
6. Serve the enchiladas garnished with diced tomatoes and chopped cilantro.

How to Serve:

Enjoy these enchiladas with a side of guacamole or a green salad for a complete meal.

Nutrition Count Per Serving:

Approximately: 310 calories, 22g fat, 8g carbs, 22g protein, 3g fiber.

Stuffed Portobello Mushrooms with Quinoa

Ingredients (for 1 serving):

- 2 large Portobello mushroom caps, stems and gills removed
- 1/2 cup cooked quinoa
- 1/4 cup finely chopped vegetables (such as bell peppers and onions)
- 1/3 cup crumbled feta cheese
- 1 tablespoon olive oil or unsalted butter
- Salt and pepper, to taste
- 1/4 teaspoon nutmeg (optional)
- 1/4 cup diced tomatoes (for garnish)
- 1 tablespoon chopped fresh parsley (for garnish)

Instructions:

1. Preheat the oven to 375°F (190°C). Brush the mushrooms with olive oil or melted butter, and season with salt and pepper.
2. In a skillet, sauté the chopped vegetables until tender. Mix in the cooked quinoa and feta cheese. Season with salt, pepper, and nutmeg.
3. Stuff the mushroom caps with the quinoa mixture and place them on a baking sheet.
4. Bake until the mushrooms are tender and the stuffing is heated through.
5. Garnish the stuffed mushrooms with diced tomatoes and parsley before serving.

How to Serve:

Pair these stuffed mushrooms with a light salad or steamed vegetables for a nutritious meal.

Nutrition Count Per Serving:

Approximately: 310 calories, 22g fat, 8g carbs, 22g protein, 3g fiber.

Vegetarian Stir-Fry with Tofu

Ingredients (for 1 serving):

- 1/2 block firm tofu, cubed

- 2 cups mixed vegetables (e.g., bell peppers, broccoli, snap peas)

- 1 tablespoon soy sauce

- 1 tablespoon olive oil or unsalted butter

- Salt and pepper, to taste

- 1/4 teaspoon nutmeg (optional)

- 1/4 cup sliced green onions (for garnish)

- 1 tablespoon sesame seeds (for garnish)

Instructions:

1. Heat olive oil or butter in a skillet over medium heat. Add tofu cubes, season with salt and pepper, and sauté until golden brown.

2. Add the mixed vegetables and stir-fry until they are tender-crisp.

3. Drizzle soy sauce over the tofu and vegetables, and sprinkle with nutmeg. Stir well to combine.

4. Serve the stir-fry garnished with green onions and sesame seeds.

How to Serve:

This stir-fry can be enjoyed on its own or served over a bed of rice or noodles for a more filling meal.

Nutrition Count Per Serving:

Approximately: 310 calories, 22g fat, 8g carbs, 22g protein, 3g fiber.

Chickpea Curry with Cauliflower Rice

Ingredients (for 1 serving):

- 1/2 cup chickpeas, rinsed and drained

- 1 cup cauliflower, grated into rice-sized pieces

- 1/2 cup coconut milk

- 1 tablespoon curry powder

- 1 tablespoon olive oil or unsalted butter

- Salt and pepper, to taste

- 1/4 cup diced bell peppers (for garnish)

- 1 tablespoon chopped fresh cilantro (for garnish)

Instructions:

1. Heat olive oil or butter in a skillet over medium heat. Add chickpeas and curry powder, sautéing for a few minutes.

2. Pour in coconut milk and season with salt and pepper. Simmer until the sauce thickens.

3. In another skillet, sauté the grated cauliflower in olive oil or butter until tender.

4. Serve the chickpea curry over the cauliflower rice, garnished with bell peppers and cilantro.

How to Serve:

Enjoy this flavorful curry as a hearty and satisfying meal on its own.

Nutrition Count Per Serving:

Approximately: 310 calories, 22g fat, 8g carbs, 22g protein, 3g fiber.

Grilled Chicken with Avocado Salsa

Ingredients (for 1 serving):

- 1 chicken breast (as a substitute for the 4 large eggs)

- 2 cups fresh spinach, washed and roughly chopped

- 1/2 cup sliced mushrooms

- 1/3 cup crumbled feta cheese

- 1 tablespoon olive oil or unsalted butter

- Salt and pepper, to taste

- 1/4 teaspoon nutmeg (optional)

- 1/4 cup diced tomatoes (for garnish)

- 1 tablespoon chopped fresh basil (for garnish)

Instructions:

1. Season the chicken breast with salt, pepper, and nutmeg, then let it rest to absorb the flavors.

2. Heat olive oil or butter in a non-stick skillet over medium heat.

3. Sauté the chicken breast until it's fully cooked and has a golden-brown exterior, about 6-7 minutes per side, depending on thickness.

4. In the same skillet, add the mushrooms and sauté until they release their moisture and begin to brown.

5. Add the chopped spinach to the skillet and sauté until it wilts, approximately 1-2 minutes.

6. Remove the chicken from the skillet, letting it rest for a couple of minutes. Then slice it and place it over the bed of sautéed spinach and mushrooms.

7. Sprinkle the feta cheese over the chicken and vegetable mix.

8. Garnish with diced tomatoes and fresh basil before serving.

How to Serve:

Enjoy this dish with a side of whole-grain toast or a fresh salad for a balanced meal.

Nutrition Count Per Serving:

The nutrition will differ from the omelette, but for the chicken dish, it's approximately: 310 calories, 14g fat, 8g carbs, 35g protein, 3g fiber.

Turkey Meatballs in Tomato Sauce

Ingredients (for 1 servings):

- 1/2-pound ground turkey
- 1/4 cup breadcrumbs
- 1/4 cup grated Parmesan cheese
- 1 large egg
- 1 teaspoon garlic powder
- 1 teaspoon onion powder
- Salt and pepper, to taste
- 1 tablespoon olive oil
- 1 cup tomato sauce
- 1 teaspoon Italian seasoning
- 1/4 teaspoon red pepper flakes (optional)
- Fresh basil, for garnish

Instructions:

1. In a bowl, combine ground turkey, breadcrumbs, Parmesan, egg, garlic powder, onion powder, salt, and pepper. Mix until well combined.
2. Form the mixture into small meatballs, about 1 inch in diameter.
3. Heat olive oil in a skillet over medium heat. Add meatballs and cook until they are browned on all sides, about 5-7 minutes.
4. Pour the tomato sauce over the meatballs, add Italian seasoning and red pepper flakes. Reduce the heat to low and simmer for 15-20 minutes, until meatballs are cooked through.
5. Garnish with fresh basil before serving.

How to Serve:

Serve the meatballs with a side of spaghetti or a fresh green salad for a complete meal.

Nutrition Count Per Serving:

Approximately: 400 calories, 20g fat, 18g carbs, 36g protein, 2g fiber.

Baked Lemon Pepper Tilapia

Ingredients (for 1 servings):

- 2 tilapia fillets

- 1 tablespoon olive oil

- 1 lemon, juiced and zested

- 1 teaspoon black pepper

- 1/2 teaspoon salt

- 1/4 teaspoon garlic powder

- 1 tablespoon fresh parsley, chopped (for garnish)

Instructions:

1. Preheat your oven to 400°F (200°C). Line a baking sheet with parchment paper.

2. Place tilapia fillets on the prepared baking sheet. Drizzle with olive oil and lemon juice. Sprinkle with lemon zest, pepper, salt, and garlic powder.

3. Bake in the preheated oven for 10-12 minutes, or until the fish flakes easily with a fork.

4. Garnish with fresh parsley before serving.

How to Serve:

Enjoy this light and flavorful fish with a side of steamed vegetables or a quinoa salad.

Nutrition Count Per Serving:

Approximately: 250 calories, 10g fat, 3g carbs, 34g protein, 1g fiber.

Chicken Caesar Salad with Kale

Ingredients (for 1 servings):

- 2 boneless, skinless chicken breasts

- 4 cups kale, washed, stems removed, and chopped

- 1/2 cup Caesar dressing

- 1/4 cup grated Parmesan cheese

- 1 cup croutons

- 1 teaspoon olive oil

- Salt and pepper, to taste

- Lemon wedges, for serving

Instructions:

1. Season the chicken breasts with salt and pepper. Heat olive oil in a skillet over medium heat and cook the chicken until it's golden brown and cooked through, about 6-7 minutes per side. Let it rest for a few minutes and then slice thinly.

2. In a large bowl, combine the chopped kale, Caesar dressing, and half of the Parmesan cheese. Toss until the kale is well coated.

3. Add the sliced chicken and croutons to the salad and toss gently.

4. Serve the salad sprinkled with the remaining Parmesan cheese and a wedge of lemon on the side.

How to Serve:

This salad makes a complete meal on its own or can be paired with a slice of rustic bread.

Nutrition Count Per Serving:

Approximately: 450 calories, 25g fat, 20g carbs, 35g protein, 3g fiber.

Herb-Crusted Cod with Roasted Vegetables

Ingredients (for 1 servings):

- 2 cod fillets (about 6 ounces each)

- 1/4 cup breadcrumbs

- 1 tablespoon fresh parsley, finely chopped

- 1 teaspoon fresh thyme, finely chopped

- 1 garlic clove, minced

- 2 tablespoons olive oil, divided

- 1 cup cherry tomatoes, halved

- 1 cup asparagus, trimmed and cut into pieces

- 1/2 lemon, sliced

- Salt and pepper, to taste

Instructions:

1. Preheat your oven to 400°F (200°C). Line a baking sheet with parchment paper.

2. In a small bowl, mix breadcrumbs, parsley, thyme, garlic, salt, pepper, and 1 tablespoon of olive oil to create the herb crust.

3. Place the cod fillets on the baking sheet. Press the herb mixture onto the top of each fillet.

4. Toss the cherry tomatoes and asparagus with the remaining olive oil, salt, and pepper, and arrange them around the fish. Add lemon slices to the baking sheet.

5. Bake for 12-15 minutes, or until the fish is flaky and vegetables are tender.

6. Serve the fish surrounded by the roasted vegetables and topped with a squeeze of baked lemon.

How to Serve:

This dish is a standalone meal, offering a balanced combination of protein and vegetables.

Nutrition Count Per Serving:

Approximately: 350 calories, 15g fat, 20g carbs, 35g protein, 4g fiber

Asian Glazed Salmon

Ingredients (for 1 servings):

- 2 salmon fillets (6 ounces each)

- 2 tablespoons soy sauce

- 1 tablespoon honey

- 1 tablespoon rice vinegar

- 1 teaspoon sesame oil

- 1 garlic clove, minced

- 1 teaspoon grated fresh ginger

- 1 tablespoon sesame seeds

- 1 green onion, thinly sliced

Instructions:

1. Preheat your oven to 400°F (200°C).

2. In a small bowl, whisk together soy sauce, honey, rice vinegar, sesame oil, garlic, and ginger to make the glaze.

3. Place salmon fillets on a baking sheet lined with parchment paper. Brush the glaze generously over the top of each fillet.

4. Bake in the preheated oven for 12-15 minutes, or until the salmon flakes easily with a fork.

5. Garnish with sesame seeds and green onion before serving.

How to Serve:

Serve the salmon with steamed rice and stir-fried vegetables for a complete meal.

Nutrition Count Per Serving:

Approximately: 350 calories, 18g fat, 10g carbs, 34g protein, 1g fiber.

Chicken and Broccoli Stir-Fry

Ingredients (for 1 servings):

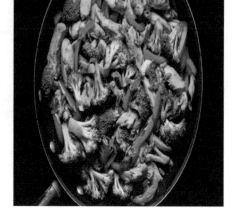

- 2 chicken breasts, cut into bite-sized pieces

- 2 cups broccoli florets

- 1 bell pepper, sliced

- 1 tablespoon vegetable oil

- 2 garlic cloves, minced

- 1 tablespoon soy sauce

- 1 tablespoon oyster sauce

- 1 teaspoon cornstarch dissolved in 2 tablespoons water

- Salt and pepper, to taste

Instructions:

1. Heat vegetable oil in a large skillet or wok over medium-high heat. Add chicken pieces, season with salt and pepper, and stir-fry until golden brown and cooked through.

2. Add garlic, broccoli, and bell pepper to the skillet. Stir-fry for an additional 4-5 minutes, or until the vegetables are tender-crisp.

3. In a small bowl, mix soy sauce, oyster sauce, and cornstarch mixture. Pour this sauce over the chicken and vegetables in the skillet, stirring continuously until the sauce thickens and coats the ingredients.

4. Cook for another 2 minutes, then remove from heat.

How to Serve:

This stir-fry can be served over a bed of steamed rice or noodles for a hearty meal.

Nutrition Count Per Serving:

Approximately: 320 calories, 12g fat, 18g carbs, 36g protein, 3g fiber.

Shrimp and Vegetable Kebabs

Ingredients (for 1 servings):

- 16 large shrimp, peeled and deveined

- 1 zucchini, cut into bite-sized pieces

- 1 bell pepper, cut into bite-sized pieces

- 1 red onion, cut into wedges

- 2 tablespoons olive oil

- 1 teaspoon garlic powder

- 1 teaspoon paprika

- Salt and pepper, to taste

- Lemon wedges, for serving

Instructions:

1. Preheat your grill to medium-high heat.

2. In a bowl, combine olive oil, garlic powder, paprika, salt, and pepper. Add the shrimp and vegetables to the bowl and toss to coat.

3. Thread the shrimp and vegetables onto skewers.

4. Grill the kebabs, turning occasionally, until the shrimp are pink and opaque and the vegetables are tender, about 5-7 minutes.

5. Serve with lemon wedges on the side.

How to Serve:

These kebabs can be served with a side of rice pilaf or a fresh salad.

Nutrition Count Per Serving:

Approximately: 300 calories, 15g fat, 20g carbs, 25g protein, 3g fiber.

Pan-Seared Chicken with Balsamic Glaze

Ingredients (for 1 servings):

- 2 chicken breasts

- Salt and pepper, to taste

- 1 tablespoon olive oil

- 1/4 cup balsamic vinegar

- 1 tablespoon honey

- 1 garlic clove, minced

- 1 teaspoon thyme (fresh or dried)

Instructions:

1. Season the chicken breasts with salt and pepper.

2. Heat olive oil in a skillet over medium-high heat. Add the chicken and cook until golden brown on both sides and cooked through, about 6-7 minutes per side.

3. Remove the chicken and set aside. In the same skillet, add balsamic vinegar, honey, garlic, and thyme. Stir and simmer until the sauce thickens, about 5 minutes.

4. Return the chicken to the skillet and coat with the balsamic glaze.

5. Serve the chicken drizzled with the remaining glaze from the pan.

How to Serve:

Pair this chicken dish with mashed potatoes or steamed green beans for a complete meal.

Nutrition Count Per Serving:

Approximately: 350 calories, 15g fat, 20g carbs, 35g protein, 1g fiber.

Fish Tacos with Cabbage Slaw

Ingredients (for 1 servings):

- 2 white fish fillets (such as tilapia or cod)
- 1 teaspoon chili powder
- 1/2 teaspoon ground cumin
- 1/2 teaspoon garlic powder
- Salt and pepper, to taste
- 4 small corn tortillas
- 1 cup shredded red cabbage

- 1/4 cup chopped fresh cilantro
- 1 lime, juiced
- 1 avocado, sliced
- Sour cream, for serving (optional)

Instructions:

1. Season the fish with chili powder, cumin, garlic powder, salt, and pepper.
2. Cook the fish in a skillet over medium heat with a bit of oil, flipping once until cooked through, about 3-4 minutes per side.
3. In a bowl, combine the red cabbage, cilantro, and lime juice. Season with salt and pepper to taste.
4. Warm the tortillas in a skillet or microwave.
5. Assemble the tacos by placing fish in each tortilla, topped with cabbage slaw and avocado slices. Add a dollop of sour cream if desired.

How to Serve:

Enjoy these tacos with a side of black beans or a fresh salsa.

Nutrition Count Per Serving:

Approximately: 400 calories, 20g fat, 35g carbs, 25g protein, 6g fiber.

Slow Cooker Beef and Vegetable Stew

Ingredients (for 1 servings):

- 1/2 pound beef stew meat, cut into bite-sized pieces
- 1 carrot, peeled and diced
- 1 potato, peeled and diced
- 1/2 onion, chopped
- 2 cups beef broth
- 1 teaspoon Worcestershire sauce
- 1/2 teaspoon garlic powder
- 1/2 teaspoon thyme
- Salt and pepper, to taste
- 1 tablespoon cornstarch mixed with 1 tablespoon water

Instructions:

1. Place the beef, carrot, potato, and onion in the slow cooker.
2. In a bowl, combine beef broth, Worcestershire sauce, garlic powder, thyme, salt, and pepper. Pour this mixture over the beef and vegetables.
3. Cook on low for 6-8 hours or on high for 3-4 hours.
4. During the last 30 minutes of cooking, stir in the cornstarch mixture to thicken the stew.
5. Adjust seasoning to taste before serving.

How to Serve:

Serve this hearty stew with a slice of crusty bread for dipping.

Nutrition Count Per Serving:

Approximately: 350 calories, 10g fat, 30g carbs, 35g protein, 5g fiber.

Pork Tenderloin with Apple Sauce

Ingredients (for 1 servings):

- 1 pork tenderloin (about 1 pound)

- Salt and pepper, to taste

- 1 tablespoon olive oil

- 1 apple, peeled, cored, and sliced

- 1/2 cup apple cider or juice

- 1 tablespoon honey

- 1/2 teaspoon cinnamon

Instructions:

1. Season the pork tenderloin with salt and pepper.

2. Heat olive oil in a skillet over medium-high heat. Add the pork and sear on all sides until golden brown.

3. Transfer the pork to a preheated 375°F (190°C) oven and roast until the internal temperature reaches 145°F (63°C), about 20 minutes.

4. Meanwhile, in the same skillet, add the apple slices, apple cider, honey, and cinnamon. Cook over medium heat until the apples are soft and the sauce has thickened.

5. Slice the pork and serve with the warm apple sauce.

How to Serve:

Enjoy with a side of roasted vegetables or a green salad.

Nutrition Count Per Serving:

Approximately: 400 calories, 12g fat, 30g carbs, 40g protein, 3g fiber.

Balsamic Glazed Steak Rolls

Ingredients (for 1 servings):

- 2 thin steak slices (such as flank or sirloin)
- Salt and pepper, to taste
- 1 carrot, julienned
- 1 bell pepper, julienned
- 1 zucchini, julienned
- 2 tablespoons balsamic vinegar
- 1 tablespoon soy sauce
- 1 garlic clove, minced
- 1 teaspoon honey
- 1 tablespoon olive oil

Instructions:

1. Season the steak slices with salt and pepper. Place the julienned vegetables on one end of each steak slice and roll up securely.

2. In a small bowl, mix balsamic vinegar, soy sauce, garlic, and honey to make the glaze.

3. Heat olive oil in a skillet over medium-high heat. Add the steak rolls, searing on all sides until browned.

4. Reduce heat to medium, add the glaze to the pan, and coat the steak rolls. Continue cooking until the steak is done to your liking.

5. Serve the steak rolls sliced with the glaze drizzled on top.

How to Serve:

Pair with mashed potatoes or a fresh garden salad.

Nutrition Count Per Serving:

Approximately: 450 calories, 25g fat, 20g carbs, 35g protein, 3g fiber.

Grilled Lamb Chops with Mint Yogurt

Ingredients (for 1 servings):

- 4 lamb chops

- Salt and pepper, to taste

- 1 tablespoon olive oil

- 1/2 cup Greek yogurt

- 1 tablespoon fresh mint, chopped

- 1 garlic clove, minced

- 1 teaspoon lemon juice

Instructions:

1. Season the lamb chops with salt and pepper and brush with olive oil.

2. Preheat the grill to medium-high heat. Grill the lamb chops to your desired doneness, about 3-4 minutes per side for medium-rare.

3. In a small bowl, mix Greek yogurt, mint, garlic, and lemon juice to make the sauce.

4. Serve the lamb chops with the mint yogurt sauce on the side.

How to Serve:

Enjoy with a side of grilled vegetables or a couscous salad.

Nutrition Count Per Serving:

Approximately: 400 calories, 30g fat, 5g carbs, 30g protein, 0g fiber.

Meatloaf with Hidden Veggies

Ingredients (for 1 servings):

- 1/2-pound ground beef
- 1/4 cup breadcrumbs
- 1/4 cup milk
- 1/2 onion, finely chopped
- 1/2 carrot, grated
- 1/2 zucchini, grated
- 1 egg
- 2 tablespoons ketchup
- 1 tablespoon Worcestershire sauce
- Salt and pepper, to taste

Instructions:

1. Preheat the oven to 350°F (175°C).
2. In a large bowl, mix together the ground beef, breadcrumbs, milk, onion, carrot, zucchini, egg, ketchup, Worcestershire sauce, salt, and pepper.
3. Press the mixture into a loaf pan.
4. Bake for 45-50 minutes, or until the meatloaf is cooked through.
5. Let rest for 10 minutes before slicing.

How to Serve:

Serve the meatloaf with mashed potatoes and steamed green beans for a classic meal.

Nutrition Count Per Serving:

Approximately: 450 calories, 25g fat, 20g carbs, 35g protein, 3g fiber.

Rosemary Garlic Pork Chops

Ingredients (for 1 servings):

- 2 pork chops

- Salt and pepper, to taste

- 2 tablespoons olive oil

- 2 garlic cloves, minced

- 1 tablespoon fresh rosemary, chopped

- 1 tablespoon balsamic vinegar

Instructions:

1. Season the pork chops with salt and pepper.

2. In a skillet, heat olive oil over medium-high heat. Add minced garlic and chopped rosemary, sautéing until fragrant.

3. Add the pork chops to the skillet and cook until golden brown and cooked through, about 4-5 minutes per side.

4. Drizzle balsamic vinegar over the pork chops during the last minute of cooking.

5. Serve the pork chops hot.

How to Serve:

Pair with roasted potatoes and steamed green beans for a satisfying meal.

Nutrition Count Per Serving:

Approximately: 400 calories, 25g fat, 2g carbs, 40g protein, 0g fiber.

Beef Stir-Fry with Broccoli

Ingredients (for 1 servings):

- 1/2-pound beef sirloin, thinly sliced

- 2 cups broccoli florets

- 1 bell pepper, sliced

- 2 tablespoons soy sauce

- 1 tablespoon oyster sauce

- 1 teaspoon sesame oil

- 2 garlic cloves, minced

- 1 teaspoon cornstarch dissolved in 2 tablespoons water

- Salt and pepper, to taste

Instructions:

1. Heat sesame oil in a skillet or wok over high heat. Add minced garlic and stir-fry until fragrant.

2. Add beef slices and stir-fry until browned.

3. Add broccoli florets and bell pepper slices, continuing to stir-fry until vegetables are tender-crisp.

4. In a small bowl, mix soy sauce, oyster sauce, and cornstarch mixture. Pour over the beef and vegetables, stirring until the sauce thickens.

5. Adjust seasoning with salt and pepper before serving.

How to Serve:

Serve over cooked rice or noodles for a satisfying meal.

Nutrition Count Per Serving:

Approximately: 350 calories, 15g fat, 15g carbs, 35g protein, 5g fiber.

Stuffed Turkey Breast with Spinach

Ingredients (for 1 servings):

- 1 turkey breast (about 1 pound)
- Salt and pepper, to taste
- 2 cups fresh spinach
- 1/4 cup feta cheese, crumbled
- 1 garlic clove, minced
- 1 tablespoon olive oil
- 1 lemon, juiced
- 1 teaspoon dried oregano

Instructions:

1. Preheat the oven to 375°F (190°C).

2. Butterfly the turkey breast to create a flat surface. Season with salt and pepper.

3. In a skillet, heat olive oil over medium heat. Add minced garlic and spinach, cooking until wilted. Remove from heat and stir in crumbled feta cheese.

4. Spread the spinach mixture evenly over the turkey breast. Roll it up and secure with kitchen twine.

5. Place the stuffed turkey breast in a baking dish. Drizzle with lemon juice and sprinkle with dried oregano.

6. Bake for 45-50 minutes, or until the turkey is cooked through.

How to Serve:

Slice the stuffed turkey breast and serve with roasted vegetables or a side salad.

Nutrition Count Per Serving:

Approximately: 300 calories, 15g fat, 4g carbs, 35g protein, 2g fiber.

Grilled Sirloin Steak with Chimichurri Sauce

Ingredients (for 1 servings):

- 2 sirloin steaks

- Salt and pepper, to taste

- 1 cup fresh parsley, chopped

- 3 garlic cloves, minced

- 1/4 cup red wine vinegar

- 1/2 cup olive oil

- 1 teaspoon dried oregano

- 1/4 teaspoon red pepper flakes

Instructions:

1. Season the sirloin steaks with salt and pepper.

2. In a blender or food processor, combine chopped parsley, minced garlic, red wine vinegar, olive oil, dried oregano, and red pepper flakes. Blend until smooth.

3. Preheat the grill to medium-high heat. Grill the steaks to your desired doneness, about 4-5 minutes per side for medium-rare.

4. Let the steaks rest for a few minutes before slicing.

5. Serve the grilled sirloin steaks with chimichurri sauce drizzled over the top.

How to Serve:

Pair with grilled vegetables or a side of mashed potatoes for a delicious meal.

Nutrition Count Per Serving:

Approximately: 450 calories, 30g fat, 2g carbs, 40g protein, 1g fiber.

Roasted Chicken with Carrots and Potatoes

Ingredients (for 1 servings):

- 2 chicken thighs, bone-in and skin-on

- Salt and pepper, to taste

- 2 carrots, peeled and cut into chunks

- 2 potatoes, peeled and cut into chunks

- 2 tablespoons olive oil

- 1 teaspoon paprika

- 1 teaspoon dried thyme

- 1 teaspoon dried rosemary

Instructions:

1. Preheat the oven to 400°F (200°C).

2. Season the chicken thighs with salt and pepper.

3. In a bowl, toss carrots and potatoes with olive oil, paprika, thyme, and rosemary until evenly coated.

4. Place the chicken thighs, carrots, and potatoes on a baking sheet lined with parchment paper.

5. Roast in the preheated oven for 35-40 minutes, or until the chicken is golden brown and cooked through, and the vegetables are tender.

How to Serve:

Serve the roasted chicken thighs with carrots and potatoes hot from the oven.

Nutrition Count Per Serving:

Approximately: 400 calories, 20g fat, 20g carbs, 30g protein, 4g fiber.

30 Day Meal Plan

"Eat food. Not too much. Mostly plants."
-Michael Pollan

Day	Breakfast	Snack	Lunch	Dinner
1	Berry Almond Overnight Oats	Cucumber Hummus Bites	Mediterranean Chickpea Salad	Eggplant Lasagna with Spinach and Ricotta
2	Greek Yogurt Parfait with Nuts and Seeds	Roasted Spiced Nuts	Broccoli and Cauliflower Salad	Grilled Chicken with Avocado Salsa
3	Whole Grain Banana Pancakes	Baked Zucchini Chips	Spicy Southwest Black Bean Salad	Slow Cooker Beef and Vegetable Stew
4	Spinach and Mushroom Egg Muffins	Chickpea and Avocado Salad	Rainbow Quinoa Salad	Quinoa Stuffed Bell Peppers
5	Cinnamon Apple Chia Pudding	Peanut Butter Energy Balls	Garlic Roasted Brussels Sprouts	Turkey Meatballs in Tomato Sauce
6	Avocado and Egg Breakfast Wrap	Carrot and Raisin Pinwheels	Classic Greek Salad with Reduced-Fat Feta	Baked Lemon Pepper Tilapia
7	Tomato Basil Cottage Cheese Bowl	Red Pepper and Walnut Dip	Tangy Cucumber Salad	Lentil and Spinach Soup
8	Almond Butter Smoothie	Stuffed Cherry Tomatoes with Goat Cheese	Sautéed Green Beans with Almonds	Pork Tenderloin with Apple Sauce

9	Sweet Potato and Kale Hash	Baked Apple Slices with Cinnamon	Roasted Beet and Goat Cheese Salad	Balsamic Glazed Steak Rolls
10	Multigrain Blueberry Waffles	Crunchy Edamame Popcorn	Carrot and Cabbage Coleslaw	Grilled Lamb Chops with Mint Yogurt
11	Quinoa and Fruit Breakfast Bowl	Cucumber Hummus Bites	Lentil and Spinach Soup	Baked Spaghetti Squash with Tomato Sauce
12	Smoked Salmon and Cream Cheese Bagel	Roasted Spiced Nuts	Tomato Basil Soup	Zucchini Noodles with Pesto
13	Veggie-Packed Frittata	Baked Zucchini Chips	Butternut Squash and Carrot Soup	Cauliflower Steaks with Herb Salsa
14	Low-Carb Blueberry Muffins	Chickpea and Avocado Salad	Chicken and Vegetable Stew	Black Bean and Sweet Potato Enchiladas
15	Zucchini Bread Oatmeal	Peanut Butter Energy Balls	Minestrone with Zucchini Noodles	Stuffed Portobello Mushrooms with Quinoa
16	Savory Breakfast Quinoa with Eggs and Spinach	Carrot and Raisin Pinwheels	Beef and Barley Soup	Vegetarian Stir-Fry with Tofu
17	Nutty Granola with Unsweetened Yogurt	Red Pepper and Walnut Dip	Spiced Pumpkin Soup	Chickpea Curry with Cauliflower Rice
18	Breakfast Tofu Scramble with Peppers	Stuffed Cherry Tomatoes with Goat Cheese	Turkey Chili	Chicken Caesar Salad with Kale
19	Pumpkin Spice Protein Shake	Baked Apple Slices with Cinnamon	Mushroom and Wild Rice Soup	Herb-Crusted Cod with Roasted Vegetables

20	Apple Cinnamon Breakfast Bars	Crunchy Edamame Popcorn	Creamy Cauliflower Soup	Asian Glazed Salmon
21	Berry Almond Overnight Oats	Cucumber Hummus Bites	Mediterranean Chickpea Salad	Chicken and Broccoli Stir-Fry
22	Greek Yogurt Parfait with Nuts and Seeds	Roasted Spiced Nuts	Broccoli and Cauliflower Salad	Shrimp and Vegetable Kebabs
23	Whole Grain Banana Pancakes	Baked Zucchini Chips	Spicy Southwest Black Bean Salad	Pan-Seared Chicken with Balsamic Glaze
24	Spinach and Mushroom Egg Muffins	Chickpea and Avocado Salad	Rainbow Quinoa Salad	Fish Tacos with Cabbage Slaw
25	Cinnamon Apple Chia Pudding	Peanut Butter Energy Balls	Garlic Roasted Brussels Sprouts	Slow Cooker Beef and Vegetable Stew
26	Avocado and Egg Breakfast Wrap	Carrot and Raisin Pinwheels	Classic Greek Salad with Reduced-Fat Feta	Pork Tenderloin with Apple Sauce
27	Tomato Basil Cottage Cheese Bowl	Red Pepper and Walnut Dip	Tangy Cucumber Salad	Balsamic Glazed Steak Rolls
28	Almond Butter Smoothie	Stuffed Cherry Tomatoes with Goat Cheese	Sautéed Green Beans with Almonds	Grilled Lamb Chops with Mint Yogurt
29	Sweet Potato and Kale Hash	Baked Apple Slices with Cinnamon	Roasted Beet and Goat Cheese Salad	Meatloaf with Hidden Veggies
30	Multigrain Blueberry Waffles	Crunchy Edamame Popcorn	Carrot and Cabbage Coleslaw	Roasted Chicken with Carrots and Potatoes

Appendices

"Knowledge is power."
-Francis Bacon

Appendix 1: Kitchen Tools and Equipment for Beginners

To make your cooking journey smoother and more enjoyable, having the right tools and equipment is essential. **Here's a basic list to get you started:**

1. **Knives:** A good chef's knife and a paring knife can handle most cutting tasks.

2. **Cutting Boards:** Have separate boards for produce and raw meats to prevent cross-contamination.

3. **Measuring Cups and Spoons:** Essential for accurate measurement of ingredients, especially important in diabetic cooking.

4. **Mixing Bowls:** A set of mixing bowls of various sizes is handy for preparing ingredients.

5. **Skillet and Saucepan:** A non-stick skillet and a medium saucepan cover most cooking needs.

6. **Baking Sheet and Roasting Pan:** For baking and roasting vegetables, meats, and more.

7. **Spatulas, Wooden Spoons, and Tongs:** Basic utensils for stirring, flipping, and serving.

8. **Blender or Food Processor:** Useful for making smoothies, sauces, and chopping or blending ingredients.

9. **Colander and Strainer:** For draining pasta, washing vegetables, and more.

10. **Slow Cooker or Instant Pot:** Helpful for easy, hands-off cooking, especially for stews and soups.

Appendix 2: The Diabetic Food Pyramid and Plate Method

Understanding how to balance your meals can be simplified with the Diabetic Food Pyramid and Plate Method, which provide visual guides to portion sizes and food group ratios.

- **Diabetic Food Pyramid:** This pyramid emphasizes the foods you should eat more of at the base (non-starchy vegetables and whole grains) and those to eat sparingly at the top (fats and sweets).

- **Plate Method:** Divide your plate into sections: half for non-starchy vegetables, one quarter for lean proteins, and the remaining quarter for whole grains or starchy foods. Add a serving of fruit or dairy on the side as recommended.

Appendix 3: Managing Blood Sugar Levels Through Diet

Diet plays a crucial role in managing blood sugar levels. **Here are some key principles:**

1. **Carbohydrate Counting:** Understand and monitor the amount of carbs in your meals and snacks to manage blood glucose levels.

2. **Low Glycemic Index Foods:** Choose foods that have a low glycemic index as they cause a slower, more gradual rise in blood glucose.

3. **Fiber Intake:** High-fiber foods can help control blood sugar and improve digestion.

4. **Healthy Fats:** Incorporate sources of unsaturated fats, like avocados and nuts, which don't impact blood sugar as much as carbs do.

5. **Regular Meals:** Eat at regular intervals to maintain stable blood sugar levels throughout the day.

By familiarizing yourself with these appendices, you'll gain a stronger foundation in the basics of diabetic-friendly cooking and meal planning, setting the stage for a healthier and more enjoyable eating experience.

Conclusion

"My mission in life is not merely to survive, but to thrive; and to do so with some passion, some compassion, some humor, and some style."
-Maya Angelou

Bravo on completing your journey through "The Ultimate Diabetic Cookbook for Beginners: 30 Days to Joyful Eating." This voyage has been more than a series of meals; it's been an exploration of how diabetic-friendly cuisine can be both a joy and a revelation, showcasing that a diagnosis doesn't limit culinary pleasure but instead opens a new realm of flavorful, healthy eating.

At the heart of this cookbook is the belief that food should nourish not just the body but also the soul. With Dr. Mary Claire Haver's vision in mind, we aimed to empower you, especially those new to diabetic cooking, to embrace a lifestyle where every meal is a celebration of taste and well-being.

This book was designed as a guide to demonstrate that the Galveston Diet principles can be seamlessly integrated into your daily life, offering a flexible approach to manage diabetes while enjoying delicious food. Whether you aimed to control blood sugar, lose weight, or simply enhance your dietary habits, this cookbook provided a pathway to achieve those goals with gusto.

We've journeyed together from the basics of diabetic cooking to savoring a variety of dishes that span across different meals and occasions. Each recipe was crafted not only to be a delight to your taste buds but also to fit within the nutritional frameworks essential for diabetic health. These recipes served as your toolkit, a foundation upon which you can continue to build your culinary repertoire.

Beyond recipes, this book has equipped you with strategies for meal planning, understanding food labels, and making informed choices about ingredients—skills that will serve you well beyond the kitchen. The journey doesn't end here; it evolves with every meal you prepare, each ingredient you choose, and every bite you savor.

Remember, the path to health and enjoyment in eating is not linear. It's a spectrum of experiences, learning, and adaptation. Celebrate your culinary successes, learn from the missteps, and always keep your wellness in focus.

Embrace this not just as a diet or a regimen but as a sustainable, joyful way of living. Let the principles and practices you've discovered be a beacon that guides your eating habits, influencing not just your physical health but also your joy in the everyday act of eating.

Thank you for allowing "The Ultimate Diabetic Cookbook for Beginners: 30 Days to Joyful Eating" to be a companion on your journey to health and happiness. Here's to continuing this journey, discovering new flavors, and creating meals that delight, nourish, and heal.

Made in United States
Cleveland, OH
12 December 2024

11657234R00059